Popular Hits
BOOK 2

Arranged by Fred Kern • Phillip Keveren • Mona Rejino

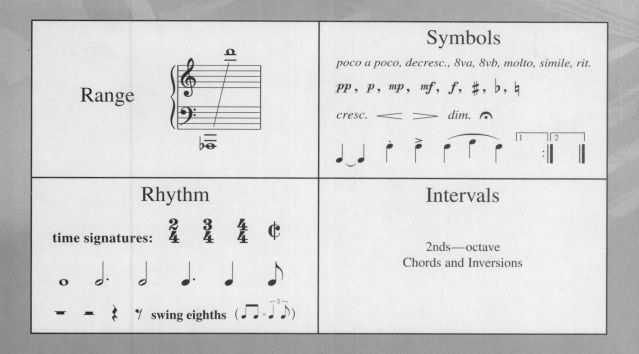

Book/CD: ISBN 978-1-4234-0937-3
Book/GM Disk: ISBN 978-1-4234-0938-0

HAL•LEONARD®
CORPORATION
7777 W. BLUEMOUND RD. P.O. BOX 13819 MILWAUKEE, WI 53213

Visit Hal Leonard Online at
www.halleonard.com

Popular Hits
BOOK 2

Suggested Order of Study:

Stand by Me

Moon River

I Will Remember You

When I'm Sixty-Four

Unchained Melody

In the Mood

Tears in Heaven

Oh, Pretty Woman

What a Wonderful World

I Write the Songs

The Phantom of the Opera

Full orchestral arrangements, included with this book on CD or GM disk, may be used for both practice and performance:

 TRACKS 9/10 The first track number is a practice tempo. The second track number is the performance tempo.

 TRACK 1 The GM disk has only one track per title and is a preset performance tempo. GM disk tracks can be slowed down to any practice tempo desired, and can also be made faster than the set tempo at will.

Contents

I Will Remember You

Theme from THE BROTHERS McMULLEN

Words and Music by Sarah McLachlan,
Seamus Egan and Dave Merenda
Arranged by Fred Kern

In the Mood

By Joe Garland
Arranged by Mona Rejino

7

I Write the Songs

Words and Music by
Bruce Johnston
Arranged by Mona Rejino

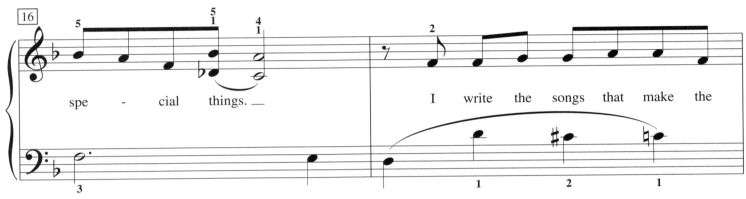

11

Moon River

from the Paramount Picture BREAKFAST AT TIFFANY'S

Words by Johnny Mercer
Music by Henry Mancini
Arranged by Phillip Keveren

(1'15")

Oh, Pretty Woman

Words and Music by Roy Orbison
and Bill Dees
Arranged by Mona Rejino

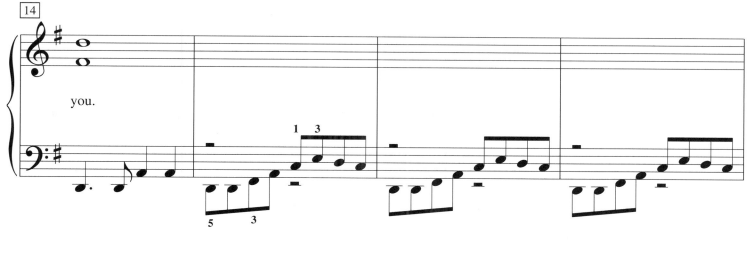

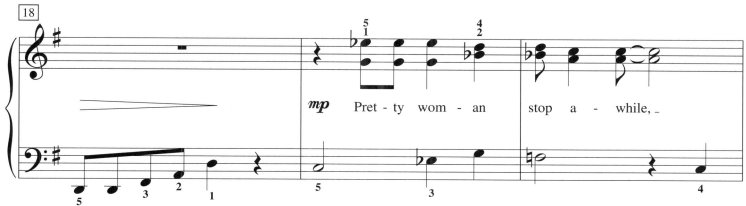

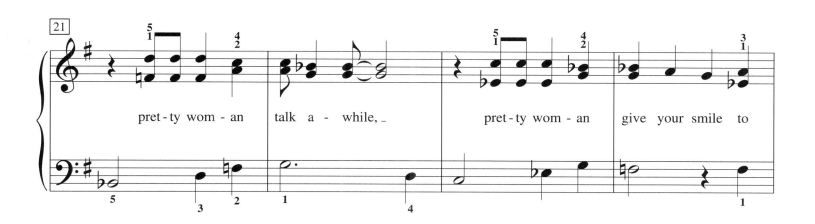

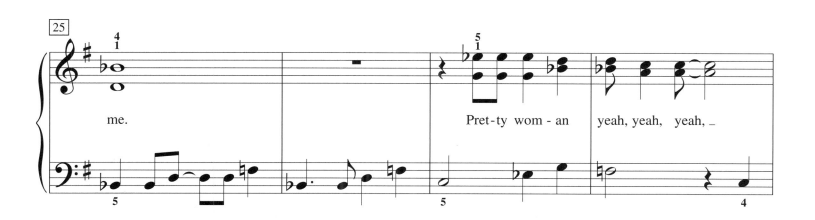

pret - ty wom - an look my way, ___ pret - ty wom - an

say you'll stay with me. ___ 'Cause I need you,

p

I'll treat you right. Come with me, ba - by.

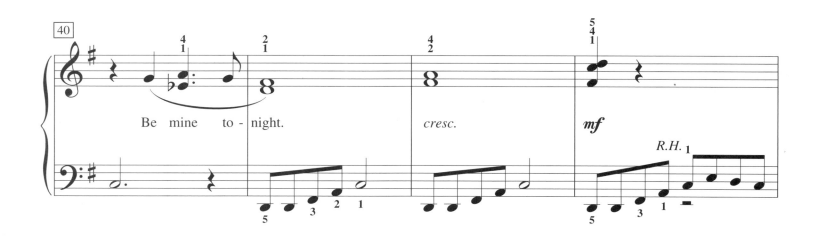

Be mine to - night. *cresc.* *mf*

R.H.

Pret-ty wom-an ___ won't you par-don me, ___ pret-ty

wom-an ___ I could-n't help but see, ___ pret-ty wom-an ___

that you look love-ly as can be. Are you lone-ly just like

me? Oh, ___ pret-ty wom-an.

The Phantom of the Opera

from THE PHANTOM OF THE OPERA

Music by Andrew Lloyd Webber
Lyrics by Charles Hart
Additional Lyrics by Richard Stilgoe and Mike Batt
Arranged by Mona Rejino

and speaks my name.
grows strong - er yet.

And do I dream a - gain?
And though you turn from me

mf

For now I find
to glance be - hind,

the phan -

- tom of the op - er - a is there

in - side my mind.

mind.

cresc. e rit.

f

Stand by Me

Words and Music by Jerry Leiber,
Mike Stoller and Ben E. King
Arranged by Phillip Keveren

Steady Rock beat (♩ = 100)   TRACKS 13/14   TRACK 7

Tears in Heaven

Words and Music by Eric Clapton
and Will Jennings
Arranged by Fred Kern

and car - ry on, 'cause I know I don't be -
through night and day, 'cause I know I just can't

long _____ here in heav-en.
stay _____ here in heav-en. *mp*

1.

2.

f Time can bring you _____

down, time can bend your knees. _____ *decresc.* *mf*

f Time can break the _____ heart, have you beg - gin' please, beg - gin'

23

please.

Both hands 8va

mp

(8va)

(8va)

Be-yond the door *mf* there's peace, I'm sure.

And I know there'll be no more tears in

heav- en. *mp* *rit.* *p*

What a Wonderful World

Words and Music by George David Weiss
and Bob Thiele
Arranged by Fred Kern

think to my-self,   "What a won - der - ful   world." _____

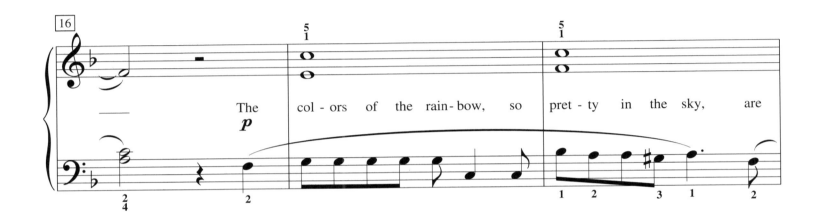

_____ The   col - ors of the rain - bow,   so   pret - ty in the sky,   are

p

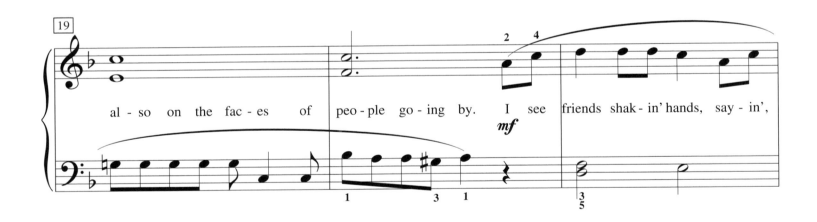

al - so on the fac - es   of   peo - ple go - ing by.   I   see   friends shak - in' hands, say - in',

mf

"How   do you do!"   They're real - ly say - in',   "I   love you."   I hear

mp

ba - bies cry,   I watch them grow;   they'll learn much more   than

I'll ev - er know, and I   think   to   my - self,   "What a won - der - ful

world."   Yes,   I   think   to   my - self,

poco a poco dim. e rit.

L.H. over

"What a won - der - ful   world." _____

Unchained Melody

much,   are   you   still   mine? _____   I

need   your   love, _____   I   need   your   love, _____   God

mf

speed   your   love _____   to   me!

p

molto rit.

pp

29

When I'm Sixty-Four

Words and Music by John Lennon
and Paul McCartney
Arranged by Fred Kern

If I'd been out ___ till quar-ter to three ___ would you lock the door? ___
Do-ing the gar - den, dig-ging the weeds, ___ who could ask for more? ___

Will you still need ___ me, will you still feed ___ me

when I'm six - ty - four?

mp

f

Send me a post - card, drop me a line ___

mf

stat - ing point of view. ___

mp

In - di - cate pre - cise - ly what you

mf